1. Hare - Hair

Hare – An animal from the rabbit family

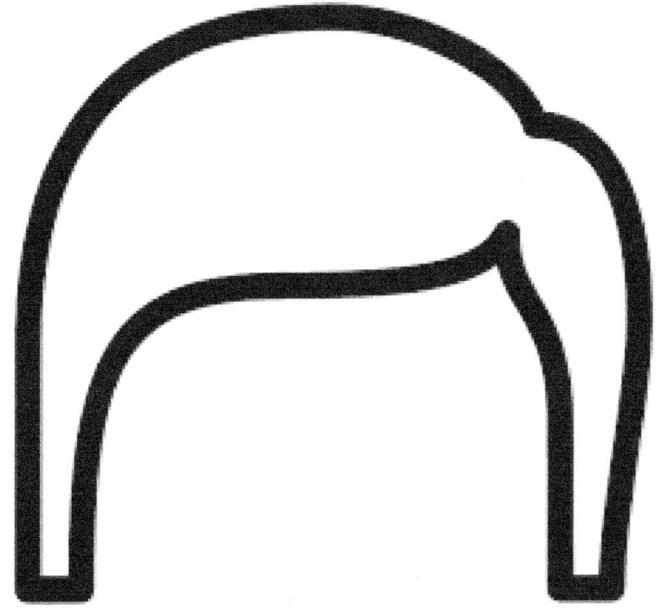

Hair – A dead part of the body of humans and ani

2. Mole - Mold

Mole – A small burrowing mammal, often confused with a platypus and is the main character for the Whacking Mole game.

Mold – Usually found on bread and fruits, a type of bacteria-plant.

3. Gnu - New

Gnu – A type of antelope-bull

New – Not old, nor damaged

4. Hoarse - Horse

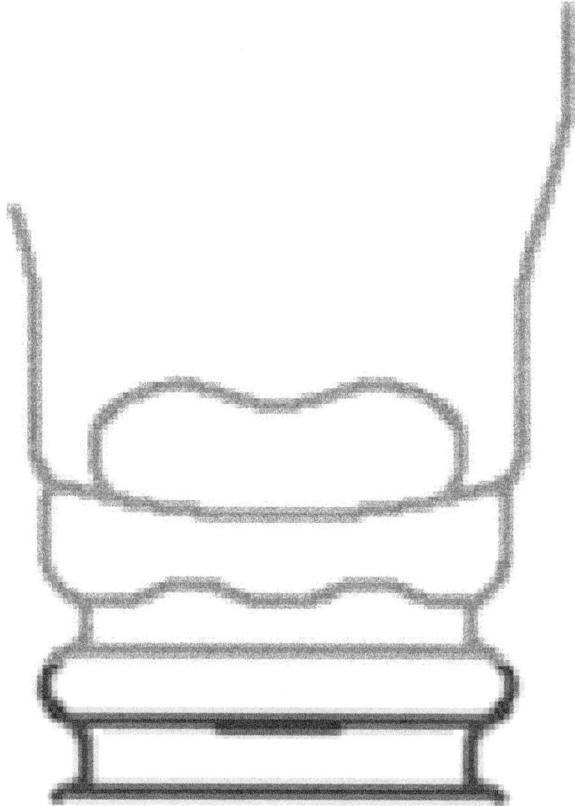

Hoarse – A harsh, big, long, rough voice.

Horse – An animal which neighs and gallops, and is used for the game Polo.

5. Wail - Whale

Wail – Cry loudly

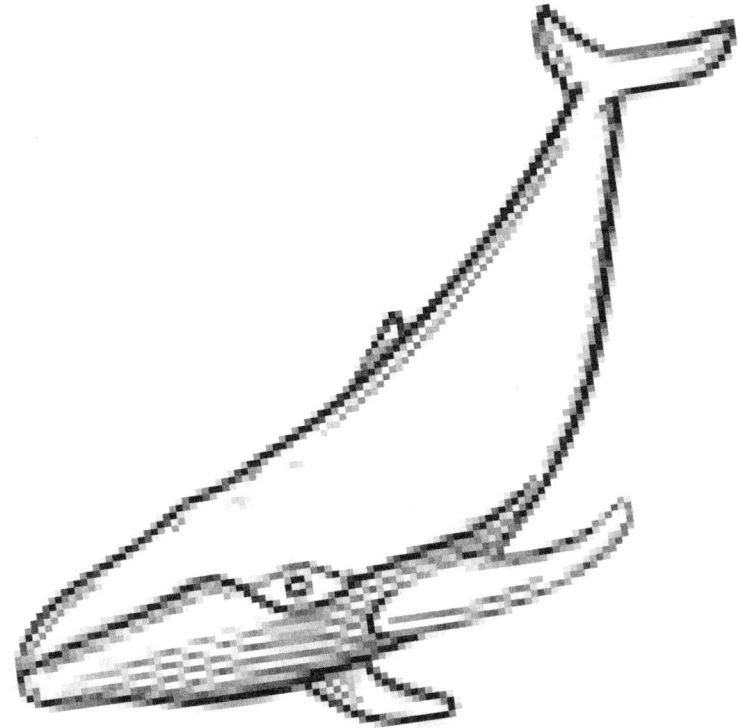

Whale – The largest mammal in the world

6. Quail - Quill

Quail – A bird

Quill – An old , historical pen, which is an old feather of a bird dipped in ink and sold to the customers.

7. Links - Lynx

Links – 1. A chain or 2. A website platformer like
https://youtube.com

Lynx – An animal from the cat family.

8. Dear - Deer

Dear – Used to address someone affectionately.

Deer – The most popular animal with antlers and main prey of carnivores.

9. Bore - Boar

Bore – Not Interesting

Boar – A wild Pig

10. Mousse - Moose

Mousse - A sweet dish made as a smooth, light mass in which the main ingredient is whipped with cream and egg white.

Moose – An animal like a big, fat antelope .

11. Meet - Meat

Meet – To know about somebody and almost always recognize each other.

Meat – the edible body parts of animals.

12. Paws - Pause

Paws – The foot of dogs , cats, chimpanzees, lions and more.

Pause – Stop

13. Fowl - Foul

Fowl – A bird of the parakeet family, often confused as a small macaw

Foul – Wrong or out

14. Caws – Cause

Caws – Sounds of a crow.

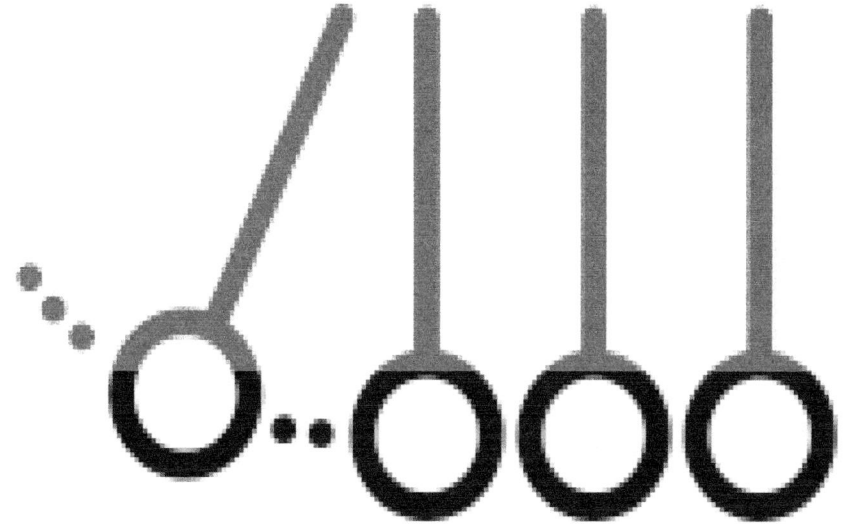

Cause – Because.

15. Roe - Row

Roe – Fish eggs, with tiny babies inside.

Row – To propel or move forward a boat with oars.

16. Heard - Herd

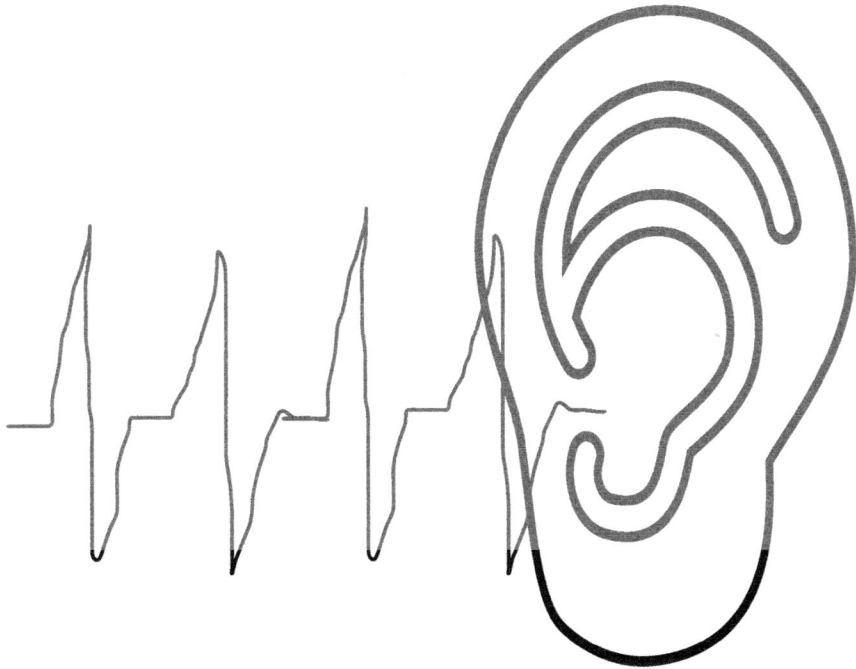

Heard – Past tense of hear.

Herd – A group of sheep, deer or antelope.

17. Fawn - Faun

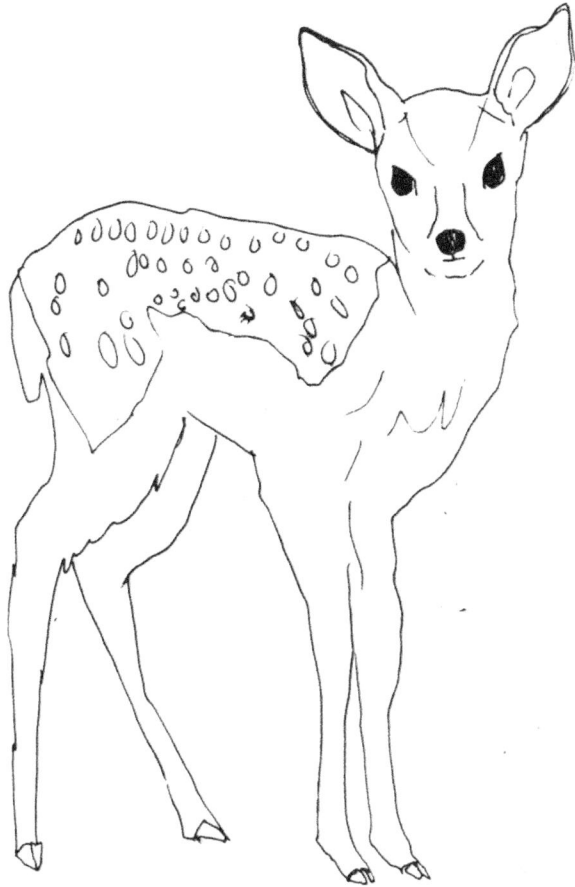

Fawn – A baby deer

Faun – A Roman or Greek mythological creature, of a half man and half goat.

18. Doe - Dough

Doe – A female deer

Dough – A thick, malleable mixture of flour and liquid, used for baking into bread or pastry.

19. Viper – Wiper

Viper – A snake

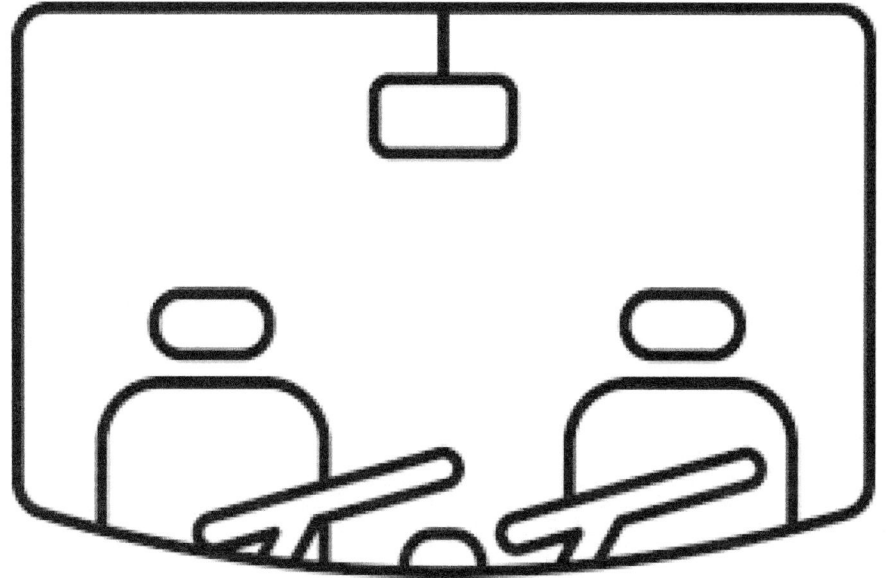

Wiper – A device for cleaning car windows.

20. Stork – Stalk

Stork – A bird

Stalk – Petiole, the main stem of an herbaceous plant often with its dependent parts.

21. Choral - Coral

Choral – Adjective form of Choir

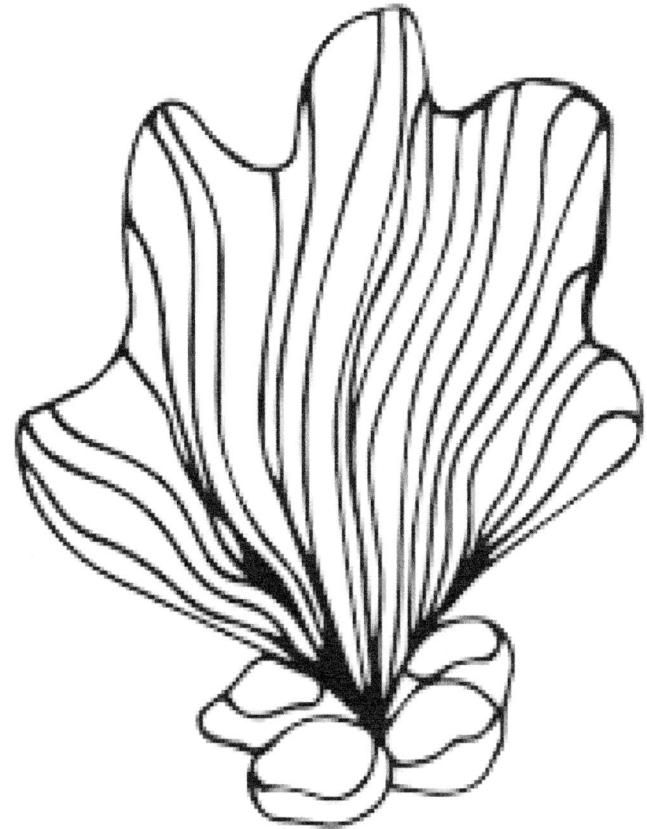

Coral – A water species that is home to fishes.

22. Flower – Flour

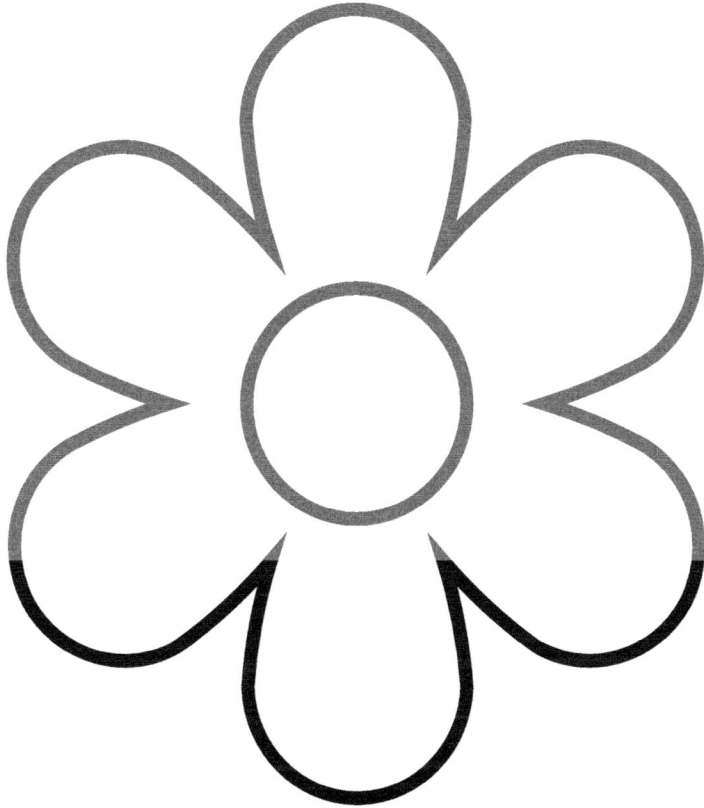

Flower – A part of a plant
that reproduces

Flour – Main ingredient for cakes and bread.

23. Pair – Pear

Pair – Two of something, often used to describe a set or couple.

Pear – A sweet and juicy fruit with a distinctive shape

24. Chili - Chilly

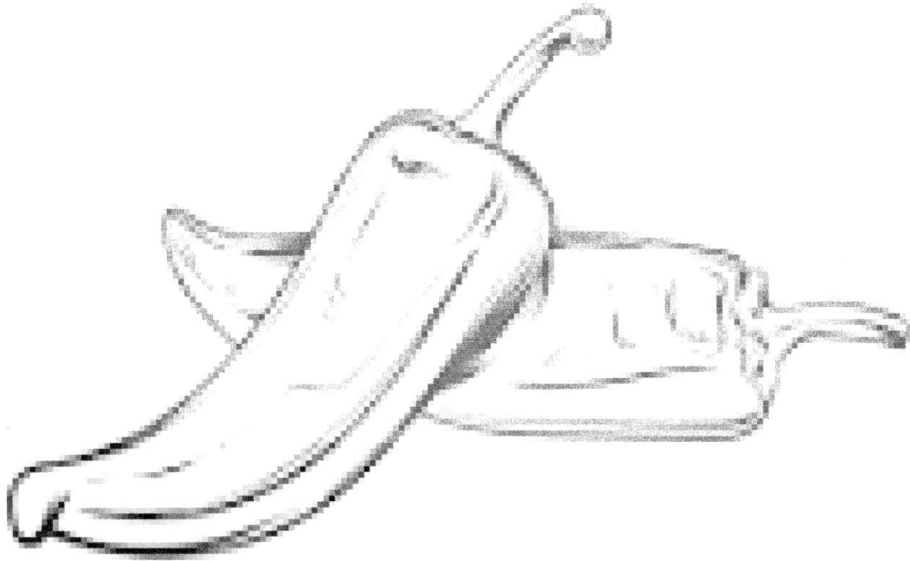

Chili – A fruit used as a vegetable.

Chilly – cold

25. Knight - Night

Knight – 1. A vital chess piece which resembles the horse and moves in an "L" shape (two steps to the front, back, left or right and one step to the right or left).

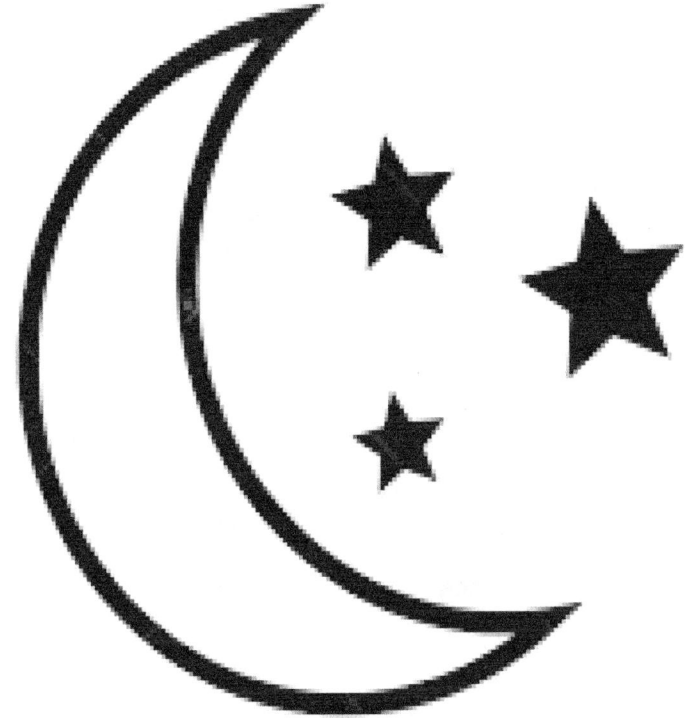

Night – A time that lasts for 7-8 hrs

What **are homophones?**
Each of two or more words having the same pronunciation but different meanings, origins, or spelling.

Types of homophones –
Homophones are broadly classified into 4 different Types - Heterograph, Heteronym, Oronym, and Synophone

Heterograph: Are the types of words that have different spellings but sound the same, Homophones in the book

Heteronyms: Are the types of words that each of two or more words which are spelled identically but have different sounds and meanings, little like homophones

Oronym: Are the type of words or phrase that sounds very much the same as another word or phrase, often as a result of sounds running together

Synophone: Are the type of words that have different meanings, different spellings, and sound similar but not the same.

Printed in Great Britain
by Amazon